MznLnx

Missing Links Exam Preps

Exam Prep for

Transnational Management

Bartlett, Ghoshal, Birkinshaw, 4th Edition

The MznLnx Exam Prep is your link from the texbook and lecture to your exams.
The MznLnx Exam Preps are unauthorized and comprehensive reviews of your textbooks.

All material provided by MznLnx and Rico Publications (c) 2010
Textbook publishers and textbook authors do not particpate in or contribute to these reviews.

MznLnx

Rico Publications

Exam Prep for Transnational Management
4th Edition
Bartlett, Ghoshal, Birkinshaw

Publisher: Raymond Houge
Assistant Editor: Michael Rouger
Text and Cover Designer: Lisa Buckner
Marketing Manager: Sara Swagger
Project Manager, Editorial Production: Jerry Emerson
Art Director: Vernon Lowerui

Product Manager: Dave Mason
Editorial Asitant: Rachel Guzmanji
Pedagogy: Debra Long
Cover Image: Jim Reed/Getty Images
Text and Cover Printer: City Printing, Inc.
Compositor: Media Mix, Inc.

(c) 2010 Rico Publications
ALL RIGHTS RESERVED. No part of this work covered by the copyright may be reproduced or used in any form or by an means--graphic, electronic, or mechanical, including photocopying, recording, taping, Web distribution, information storage, and retrieval systems, or in any other manner--without the written permission of the publisher.

Printed in the United States
ISBN:

> For more information about our products, contact us at:
> Dave.Mason@RicoPublications.com
>
> For permission to use material from this text or product, submit a request online to:
> Dave.Mason@RicoPublications.com

Contents

CHAPTER 1
Expanding Abroad: Motivations, Means, and Mentalities — 1

CHAPTER 2
Managing Conflicting Demands: Global Integration, Local Responsiveness — 5

CHAPTER 3
Developing Strategic Capabilities: Building Layers of Competitive Advantage — 16

CHAPTER 4
Developing Coordination and Control: The Organizational Challenge — 28

CHAPTER 5
Creating and Leveraging Knowledge: The Worldwide Learning Challenge — 34

CHAPTER 6
Managing across Boundaries: The Collaborative Challenge — 41

CHAPTER 7
Building Multidimensional Capabilities: The Management Challenge — 48

CHAPTER 8
Preparing for the Future: Evolution of the Transnational — 52

ANSWER KEY — 59

TO THE STUDENT

COMPREHENSIVE

The *MznLnx* Exam Prep series is designed to help you pass your exams. Editors at MznLnx review your textbooks and then prepare these practice exams to help you master the textbook material. Unlike study guides, workbooks, and practice tests provided by the texbook publisher and textbook authors, *MznLnx* gives you **all** of the material in each chapter in exam form, not just samples, so you can be sure to nail your exam.

MECHANICAL

The MznLnx Exam Prep series creates exams that will help you learn the subject matter as well as test you on your understanding. Each question is designed to help you master the concept. Just working through the exams, you gain an understanding of the subject--its a simple mechanical process that produces success.

INTEGRATED STUDY GUIDE AND REVIEW

MznLnx is not just a set of exams designed to test you, its also a comprehensive review of the subject content. Each exam question is also a review of the concept, making sure that you will get the answer correct without having to go to other sources of material. You learn as you go! Its the easiest way to pass an exam.

HUMOR

Studying can be tedious and dry. MznLnx's instructional design includes moderate humor within the exam questions on occassion, to break the tedium and revitalize the brain

Chapter 1. Expanding Abroad: Motivations, Means, and Mentalities   1

1. A _____ or transnational corporation is a corporation or enterprise that manages production or delivers services in more than one country. It can also be referred to as an international corporation.

   The first modern _____ is generally thought to be the Dutch East India Company, established in 1602.

   a. Command center
   b. Small and medium enterprises
   c. Financial Accounting Standards Board
   d. Multinational corporation

2. _____ is the branch of economics that studies the dynamics of exchange rates, foreign investment, and how these affect international trade. It also studies international projects, international investments and capital flows, and trade deficits. It includes the study of futures, options and currency swaps.
   a. AAAI
   b. A4e
   c. A Stake in the Outcome
   d. International finance

3. In statistics, _____ is:

   - the arithmetic _____
   - the expected value of a random variable, which is also called the population _____.

   It is sometimes stated that the '_____' _____s average. This is incorrect if '_____' is taken in the specific sense of 'arithmetic _____' as there are different types of averages: the _____, median, and mode. Other simple statistical analyses use measures of spread, such as range, interquartile range, or standard deviation. For a real-valued random variable X, the _____ is the expectation of X. Note that not every probability distribution has a defined _____; see the Cauchy distribution for an example.

   a. Control chart
   b. Correlation
   c. Statistical inference
   d. Mean

4. A _____ is a name or trademark connected with a product or producer. _____s have become increasingly important components of culture and the economy, now being described as 'cultural accessories and personal philosophies'.

   Some people distinguish the psychological aspect of a _____ from the experiential aspect.

a. Brand extension
b. Brand loyalty
c. Brand
d. Brand awareness

5. A _____ is a framework for creating economic, social, and/or other forms of value. The term _____ is thus used for a broad range of informal and formal descriptions to represent core aspects of a business, including purpose, offerings, strategies, infrastructure, organizational structures, trading practices, and operational processes and policies.

Conceptualizations of _____s try to formalize informal descriptions into building blocks and their relationships.

a. Business networking
b. Gap analysis
c. Business model design
d. Business model

6. _____ comprises a range of practices used in an organisation to identify, create, represent, distribute and enable adoption of insights and experiences. Such insights and experiences comprise knowledge, either embodied in individuals or embedded in organisational processes or practice.

An established discipline since 1991, _____ includes courses taught in the fields of business administration, information systems, management, and library and information sciences.

a. 28-hour day
b. Knowledge management
c. 33 Strategies of War
d. 1990 Clean Air Act

7. _____ is the principle that the government must respect all of the legal rights that are owed to a person according to the law of the land. As developed through a large body of case law in the United States, this principle gives individuals a varying ability to enforce their rights against alleged violations by governments and their agents (that is, state actors), but normally not against other private citizens.

_____ has also been frequently interpreted as placing limitations on laws and legal proceedings, in order for judges instead of legislators to define and guarantee fundamental fairness, justice, and liberty.

a. Due process
b. Maximum medical improvement
c. Sick leave
d. Clayton Antitrust Act

8. _____ denotes the location where most, if not all, of the important functions of an organization are coordinated. The corporate _____ is the entity at the top of a corporation taking full responsibility managing all business activities. In the UK, the term 'head office' is most commonly used for the HQs of large corporations.

a. Command center
b. Wells Fargo ' Co.
c. National Center for Trauma-Informed Care
d. Headquarters

9. _____ is the principle of organization of a region around several political, social or financial centres. An example of a polycentric city is the Ruhr area in Germany: Today, the area is a large city that grew from a dozen smaller cities. As a result, the 'city' has no single centre, but several.

a. 33 Strategies of War
b. 28-hour day
c. 1990 Clean Air Act
d. Polycentrism

10. In economics, business, retail, and accounting, a _____ is the value of money that has been used up to produce something, and hence is not available for use anymore. In economics, a _____ is an alternative that is given up as a result of a decision. In business, the _____ may be one of acquisition, in which case the amount of money expended to acquire it is counted as _____.

a. Cost overrun
b. Cost allocation
c. Fixed costs
d. Cost

11. In decision theory and estimation theory, the _____ of an estimator, $\hat{\theta}$, of an unknown parameter of the distribution, θ, is the expected value of the loss function

$$R(\theta, \hat{\theta}) = \mathbb{E}_\theta L(\theta, \hat{\theta}) = \int L(\theta, \hat{\theta})\, dP_\theta.$$

where dP_θ is a probability measure parametrized by θ.

- For a scalar parameter θ and a quadratic loss function,

$$L(\theta, \hat{\theta}) = (\theta - \hat{\theta})^2$$

the _____ function becomes the mean squared error of the estimate,

$$R(\theta, \hat{\theta}) = E_\theta (\theta - \hat{\theta})^2$$

- In density estimation, the unknown parameter is probability density itself. The loss function is typically chosen to be a norm in an appropriate function space. For example, for L^2 norm,

$$L(f, \hat{f}) = \|f - \hat{f}\|_2^2$$

the _____ function becomes the mean integrated squared error

$$R(f, \hat{f}) = E\|f - \hat{f}\|^2$$

a. Financial modeling
b. Risk aversion
c. Linear model
d. Risk

12. _____ is the advantage gained by the initial occupant of a market segment. This advantage may stem from the fact that the first entrant can gain control of resources that followers may not be able to match. Sometimes the first mover is not able to capitalise on its advantage, leaving the opportunity for another firm to gain second-mover advantage.
a. Horizontal integration
b. Business ecosystem
c. Customer retention
d. First-mover advantage

Chapter 2. Managing Conflicting Demands: Global Integration, Local Responsiveness

1. _____ in its literal sense is the process of transformation of local or regional phenomena into global ones. It can be described as a process by which the people of the world are unified into a single society and function together.

This process is a combination of economic, technological, sociocultural and political forces.

   a. Collaborative Planning, Forecasting and Replenishment
   b. Globalization
   c. Histogram
   d. Cost Management

2. In economics, _____ is the desire to own something and the ability to pay for it. The term _____ signifies the ability or the willingness to buy a particular commodity at a given point of time.
   a. 33 Strategies of War
   b. Demand
   c. 1990 Clean Air Act
   d. 28-hour day

3. _____, in microeconomics, are the cost advantages that a business obtains due to expansion. They are factors that cause a producer's average cost per unit to fall as scale is increased. _____ is a long run concept and refers to reductions in unit cost as the size of a facility, or scale, increases.
   a. A4e
   b. Economies of scope
   c. Economies of scale
   d. A Stake in the Outcome

4. The _____ was a period in the late 18th and early 19th centuries when major changes in agriculture, manufacturing, mining, and transportation had a profound effect on the socioeconomic and cultural conditions in Britain. The changes subsequently spread throughout Europe, North America, and eventually the world. The onset of the _____ marked a major turning point in human society; almost every aspect of daily life was eventually influenced in some way.
   a. Industrial Revolution
   b. Abraham Harold Maslow
   c. Adam Smith
   d. Affiliation

5. Network externalities resemble economies of scale, but they are not considered such because they are a function of the number of users of a good or service in an industry, not of the production efficiency within a business. _____ are only considered examples of network externalities if they are driven by demand side economies.

Chapter 2. Managing Conflicting Demands: Global Integration, Local Responsiveness

Formally, a production function is defined to have:

- constant returns to scale if (for any constant a greater than or equal to 0)
- increasing returns to scale if (for any constant a greater than 1)
- decreasing returns to scale if (for any constant a greater than 1)

where K and L are factors of production, capital and labour, respectively.

As an example, the Cobb-Douglas functional form has constant returns to scale when the sum of the exponents adds up to one.

   a. AAAI
   b. A Stake in the Outcome
   c. A4e
   d. Economies of scale external to the firm

6. In economics, business, retail, and accounting, a _____ is the value of money that has been used up to produce something, and hence is not available for use anymore. In economics, a _____ is an alternative that is given up as a result of a decision. In business, the _____ may be one of acquisition, in which case the amount of money expended to acquire it is counted as _____.
   a. Cost allocation
   b. Cost
   c. Cost overrun
   d. Fixed costs

7. _____ are conceptually similar to economies of scale. Whereas economies of scale primarily refer to efficiencies associated with supply-side changes, such as increasing or decreasing the scale of production, of a single product type, _____ refer to efficiencies primarily associated with demand-side changes, such as increasing or decreasing the scope of marketing and distribution, of different types of products. _____ are one of the main reasons for such marketing strategies as product bundling, product lining, and family branding.
   a. Economies of scope
   b. A4e
   c. Economies of scale
   d. A Stake in the Outcome

Chapter 2. Managing Conflicting Demands: Global Integration, Local Responsiveness

8. The _____ was the outcome of the failure of negotiating governments to create the International Trade Organization (ITO.) GATT was formed in 1947 and lasted until 1994, when it was replaced by the World Trade Organization. The Bretton Woods Conference had introduced the idea for an organization to regulate trade as part of a larger plan for economic recovery after World War II.
   a. 1990 Clean Air Act
   b. 28-hour day
   c. Multilateral treaty
   d. General Agreement on Tariffs and Trade

9. Procter is a surname, and may also refer to:

   - Bryan Waller Procter (pseud. Barry Cornwall), English poet
   - Goodwin Procter, American law firm
   - _____, consumer products multinational

   a. Strict liability
   b. Downstream
   c. Procter ' Gamble
   d. Master and Servant Acts

10. In economics and game theory, _____ are games of incomplete information where players receive possibly-correlated signals of the underlying state of the world. _____ were originally defined by Carlsson and van Damme (1993.) The most important practical application of _____ has been the study of crises in financial markets such as bank runs, currency crises, and bubbles .
    a. Mixed strategy
    b. Perfect information
    c. Transferable utility
    d. Global games

11. A _____ or transnational corporation is a corporation or enterprise that manages production or delivers services in more than one country. It can also be referred to as an international corporation.

The first modern _____ is generally thought to be the Dutch East India Company, established in 1602.

Chapter 2. Managing Conflicting Demands: Global Integration, Local Responsiveness

a. Financial Accounting Standards Board
b. Small and medium enterprises
c. Command center
d. Multinational corporation

12. In economics, _____ describes the state of a market with respect to competition.

- Perfect competition, in which the market consists of a very large number of firms producing a homogeneous product.
- Monopolistic competition where there are a large number of independent firms which have a very small proportion of the market share.
- Oligopoly, in which a market is dominated by a small number of firms which own more than 40% of the market share.
- Oligopsony, a market dominated by many sellers and a few buyers.
- Monopoly, where there is only one provider of a product or service.
- Natural monopoly, a monopoly in which economies of scale cause efficiency to increase continuously with the size of the firm. A firm is a natural monopoly if it is able to serve the entire market demand at a lower cost than any combination of two or more smaller, more specialized firms.
- Monopsony, when there is only one buyer in a market.

The imperfectly competitive structure is quite identical to the realistic market conditions where some monopolistic competitors, monopolists, oligopolists, and duopolists exist and dominate the market conditions. The elements of _____ include the number and size distribution of firms, entry conditions, and the extent of differentiation.

These somewhat abstract concerns tend to determine some but not all details of a specific concrete market system where buyers and sellers actually meet and commit to trade.

a. Leading indicator
b. Productivity management
c. Deflation
d. Market structure

13. _____ is one of the managerial functions like planning, organizing, staffing and directing. It is an important function because it helps to check the errors and to take the corrective action so that deviation from standards are minimized and stated goals of the organization are achieved in desired manner. According to modern concepts, _____ is a foreseeing action whereas earlier concept of _____ was used only when errors were detected. _____ in management means setting standards, measuring actual performance and taking corrective action.

a. Schedule of reinforcement
b. Turnover
c. Decision tree pruning
d. Control

Chapter 2. Managing Conflicting Demands: Global Integration, Local Responsiveness   9

14. A _____ is a compensation, usually financial, received by a worker in exchange for their labor.

Compensation in terms of _____s is given to worker and compensation in terms of salary is given to employees. Compensation is a monetary benefits given to employees in returns of the services provided by them.

   a. Performance-related pay
   b. State Compensation Insurance Fund
   c. Profit-sharing agreement
   d. Wage

15. Various _____ can be employed dependent on the culture of the business, the nature of the task, the nature of the workforce and the personality and skills of the leaders. This idea was further developed by Robert Tannenbaum and Warren H. Schmidt (1958, 1973) who argued that the style of leadership is dependent upon the prevailing circumstance; therefore leaders should exercise a range of leadership styles and should deploy them as appropriate.

An Autocratic or authoritarian manager makes all the decisions, keeping the information and decision making among the senior management.

   a. 28-hour day
   b. Management styles
   c. 1990 Clean Air Act
   d. 33 Strategies of War

16. _____ is a theory of management that analyzes and synthesizes workflows, with the objective of improving labour productivity. The core ideas of the theory were developed by Frederick Winslow Taylor in the 1880s and 1890s, and were first published in his monographs, Shop Management and The Principles of _____ Taylor believed that decisions based upon tradition and rules of thumb should be replaced by precise procedures developed after careful study of an individual at work.
   a. Master production schedule
   b. Capacity planning
   c. Value engineering
   d. Scientific management

17. _____, widely known as F. W. Taylor, was an American mechanical engineer who sought to improve industrial efficiency. He is regarded as the father of scientific management, and was one of the first management consultants.

Taylor was one of the intellectual leaders of the Efficiency Movement and his ideas, broadly conceived, were highly influential in the Progressive Era.

Chapter 2. Managing Conflicting Demands: Global Integration, Local Responsiveness

a. Jonah Jacob Goldberg
b. Geoffrey Colvin
c. Douglas N. Daft
d. Frederick Winslow Taylor

18. The _____ captures an expanded spectrum of values and criteria for measuring organizational success: economic, ecological and social. With the ratification of the United Nations and ICLEI _____ standard for urban and community accounting in early 2007, this became the dominant approach to public sector full cost accounting. Similar UN standards apply to natural capital and human capital measurement to assist in measurements required by _____, e.g. the ecoBudget standard for reporting ecological footprint.
   a. Triple bottom line
   b. 1990 Clean Air Act
   c. 33 Strategies of War
   d. 28-hour day

19. A _____ structured in a way such that every entity in the organization, except one, is subordinate to a single other entity. This is the dominant mode of organization among large organizations; most corporations, governments, and organized religions are _____s. Hierarchies denote a singular/group of power at the top, a number of assistants underneath and hundreds of servants beneath them.
   a. Catfish effect
   b. CPS Model
   c. Matrix management
   d. Hierarchical organization

20. An _____, or organogram(me)) is a diagram that shows the structure of an organization and the relationships and relative ranks of its parts and positions/jobs. The term is also used for similar diagrams, for example ones showing the different elements of a field of knowledge or a group of languages. The French Encyclopédie had one of the first _____s of knowledge in general.
   a. A4e
   b. AAAI
   c. A Stake in the Outcome
   d. Organizational chart

21. A _____ is the belief that there is a technique, method, process, activity, incentive or reward that is more effective at delivering a particular outcome than any other technique, method, process, etc. The idea is that with proper processes, checks, and testing, a desired outcome can be delivered with fewer problems and unforeseen complications. _____s can also be defined as the most efficient (least amount of effort) and effective (best results) way of accomplishing a task, based on repeatable procedures that have proven themselves over time for large numbers of people.

Chapter 2. Managing Conflicting Demands: Global Integration, Local Responsiveness 11

a. Best practice
b. Fix it twice
c. Design management
d. Hierarchical organization

22. _____ is a term used to describe persistent social, corporate or institutional culture that avoids using or buying already existing products, research or knowledge because of its different origins. It is normally used in a pejorative sense.

As a social phenomenon, '_____' syndrome is manifested as an unwillingness to adopt an idea or product because it originates from another culture, a form of nationalism.

a. 28-hour day
b. 1990 Clean Air Act
c. 33 Strategies of War
d. Not Invented Here

23. In economics, _____ refers to the ability of a person or a country to produce a particular good at a lower marginal cost and opportunity cost than another person or country. It is the ability to produce a product most efficiently given all the other products that could be produced. It can be contrasted with absolute advantage which refers to the ability of a person or a country to produce a particular good at a lower absolute cost than another.

a. 1990 Clean Air Act
b. Comparative advantage
c. 33 Strategies of War
d. 28-hour day

24. _____ refers to metrics and measures of output from production processes, per unit of input. Labor _____, for example, is typically measured as a ratio of output per labor-hour, an input. _____ may be conceived of as a metrics of the technical or engineering efficiency of production.

a. Remanufacturing
b. Value engineering
c. Productivity
d. Master production schedule

25. A _____ is typically described as a deliberate plan of action to guide decisions and achieve rational outcome(s.) However, the term may also be used to denote what is actually done, even though it is unplanned.

The term may apply to government, private sector organizations and groups, and individuals.

Chapter 2. Managing Conflicting Demands: Global Integration, Local Responsiveness

   a. 1990 Clean Air Act
   b. 28-hour day
   c. 33 Strategies of War
   d. Policy

26. _____ or Corpocracy is a form of government where a corporation, a group of corporations or government entities with private components control the direction and governance of a country.

A historical example of _____ is the East India Company. This British trade organization ruled over most of India, with the support of the British Empire, starting from the end of 18th century until mid-19th century.

   a. 33 Strategies of War
   b. 1990 Clean Air Act
   c. 28-hour day
   d. Corporatocracy

27. A _____ is a framework for creating economic, social, and/or other forms of value. The term _____ is thus used for a broad range of informal and formal descriptions to represent core aspects of a business, including purpose, offerings, strategies, infrastructure, organizational structures, trading practices, and operational processes and policies.

Conceptualizations of _____s try to formalize informal descriptions into building blocks and their relationships.

   a. Business model design
   b. Gap analysis
   c. Business networking
   d. Business model

28. A _____ is a name or trademark connected with a product or producer. _____s have become increasingly important components of culture and the economy, now being described as 'cultural accessories and personal philosophies'.

Some people distinguish the psychological aspect of a _____ from the experiential aspect.

Chapter 2. Managing Conflicting Demands: Global Integration, Local Responsiveness

a. Brand extension
b. Brand
c. Brand loyalty
d. Brand awareness

29. _____ is the application of marketing techniques to a specific product, product line, or brand. It seeks to increase the product's perceived value to the customer and thereby increase brand franchise and brand equity. Marketers see a brand as an implied promise that the level of quality people have come to expect from a brand will continue with future purchases of the same product.
   a. Brand management
   b. Brand loyalty
   c. Brand extension
   d. Brand names

30. _____ is the science, art and technology of enclosing or protecting products for distribution, storage, sale, and use. _____ also refers to the process of design, evaluation, and production of packages. _____ can be described as a coordinated system of preparing goods for transport, warehousing, logistics, sale, and end use.
   a. Supply chain management
   b. Packaging
   c. Supply chain
   d. Wholesalers

31. _____ can be defined as the idea generation, concept development, testing and manufacturing or implementation of a physical object or service. _____ers conceptualize and evaluate ideas, making them tangible through products in a more systematic approach. The role of a _____er encompasses many characteristics of the marketing manager, product manager, industrial designer and design engineer.
   a. Product design
   b. Affiliation
   c. Abraham Harold Maslow
   d. Adam Smith

32. _____ is one of the four elements of marketing mix. An organization or set of organizations (go-betweens) involved in the process of making a product or service available for use or consumption by a consumer or business user.

The other three parts of the marketing mix are product, pricing, and promotion.

14 *Chapter 2. Managing Conflicting Demands: Global Integration, Local Responsiveness*

a. Missing completely at random
b. Distribution
c. Job creation programs
d. Matching theory

33. _____ has been described as the 'process of social influence in which one person can enlist the aid and support of others in the accomplishment of a common task'. A definition more inclusive of followers comes from Alan Keith of Genentech who said '_____ is ultimately about creating a way for people to contribute to making something extraordinary happen.'

_____ is one of the most salient aspects of the organizational context. However, defining _____ has been challenging.

a. 28-hour day
b. 1990 Clean Air Act
c. Leadership
d. Situational leadership

34. An _____ is a person temporarily or permanently residing in a country and culture other than that of the person's upbringing or legal residence. The word comes from the Latin ex and patria (country, fatherland.)

The term is sometimes used in the context of Westerners living in non-Western countries, although it is also used to describe Westerners living in other Western countries, such as Americans living in the United Kingdom, or Britons living in Spain.

a. A4e
b. AAAI
c. A Stake in the Outcome
d. Expatriate

35. A _____ is an entity formed between two or more parties to undertake economic activity together. The parties agree to create a new entity by both contributing equity, and they then share in the revenues, expenses, and control of the enterprise. The venture can be for one specific project only, or a continuing business relationship such as the Fuji Xerox _____.
a. Meritor Savings Bank v. Vinson
b. Patent
c. Civil Rights Act of 1991
d. Joint venture

36. An _____ is a person who has possession of an enterprise and assumes significant accountability for the inherent risks and the outcome. It is an ambitious leader who combines land, labor, and capital to create and market new goods or services. The term is a loanword from French and was first defined by the Irish economist Richard Cantillon.
   a. A4e
   b. AAAI
   c. A Stake in the Outcome
   d. Entrepreneur

16   Chapter 3. Developing Strategic Capabilities: Building Layers of Competitive Advantage

1. _____ is, in very basic words, a position a firm occupies against its competitors.

According to Michael Porter, the three methods for creating a sustainable _____ are through:

1. Cost leadership

2. Differentiation

3. Focus (economics)

   a. Competitive advantage
   b. 28-hour day
   c. 1990 Clean Air Act
   d. Theory Z

2. In economics and game theory, _____ are games of incomplete information where players receive possibly-correlated signals of the underlying state of the world. _____ were originally defined by Carlsson and van Damme (1993.) The most important practical application of _____ has been the study of crises in financial markets such as bank runs, currency crises, and bubbles .
   a. Perfect information
   b. Mixed strategy
   c. Transferable utility
   d. Global games

3. In decision theory and estimation theory, the _____ of an estimator, $\hat{\theta}$, of an unknown parameter of the distribution, θ, is the expected value of the loss function

$$R(\theta, \hat{\theta}) = \mathbb{E}_\theta L(\theta, \hat{\theta}) = \int L(\theta, \hat{\theta}) \, dP_\theta.$$

Chapter 3. Developing Strategic Capabilities: Building Layers of Competitive Advantage

where dP_θ is a probability measure parametrized by θ.

- For a scalar parameter θ and a quadratic loss function,

$$L(\theta, \hat{\theta}) = (\theta - \hat{\theta})^2$$

the _____ function becomes the mean squared error of the estimate,

$$R(\theta, \hat{\theta}) = E_\theta(\theta - \hat{\theta})^2$$

- In density estimation, the unknown parameter is probability density itself. The loss function is typically chosen to be a norm in an appropriate function space. For example, for L^2 norm,

$$L(f, \hat{f}) = \|f - \hat{f}\|_2^2$$

the _____ function becomes the mean integrated squared error

$$R(f, \hat{f}) = E\|f - \hat{f}\|^2$$

a. Linear model
b. Financial modeling
c. Risk aversion
d. Risk

4. _____, in microeconomics, are the cost advantages that a business obtains due to expansion. They are factors that cause a producer's average cost per unit to fall as scale is increased. _____ is a long run concept and refers to reductions in unit cost as the size of a facility, or scale, increases.
   a. A Stake in the Outcome
   b. Economies of scope
   c. A4e
   d. Economies of scale

5. Network externalities resemble economies of scale, but they are not considered such because they are a function of the number of users of a good or service in an industry, not of the production efficiency within a business. _____ are only considered examples of network externalities if they are driven by demand side economies.

Chapter 3. Developing Strategic Capabilities: Building Layers of Competitive Advantage

Formally, a production function ⬚> is defined to have:

- constant returns to scale if (for any constant a greater than or equal to 0) ⬚>
- increasing returns to scale if (for any constant a greater than 1) ⬚>
- decreasing returns to scale if (for any constant a greater than 1) ⬚>

where K and L are factors of production, capital and labour, respectively.

As an example, the Cobb-Douglas functional form has constant returns to scale when the sum of the exponents adds up to one.

a. AAAI
b. A4e
c. A Stake in the Outcome
d. Economies of scale external to the firm

6. In statistics, _____ is:

- the arithmetic _____
- the expected value of a random variable, which is also called the population _____.

It is sometimes stated that the '_____' _____s average. This is incorrect if '_____' is taken in the specific sense of 'arithmetic _____' as there are different types of averages: the _____, median, and mode. Other simple statistical analyses use measures of spread, such as range, interquartile range, or standard deviation. For a real-valued random variable X, the _____ is the expectation of X. Note that not every probability distribution has a defined _____; see the Cauchy distribution for an example.

a. Correlation
b. Control chart
c. Statistical inference
d. Mean

7. _____ is an American writer on business management practices, best-known for, In Search of Excellence (co-authored with Robert H. Waterman, Jr.)

Peters was born in Baltimore, Maryland. He went to Severn School for High School and attended Cornell University, receiving a bachelor's degree in civil engineering in 1965, and a master's degree in 1966.

Chapter 3. Developing Strategic Capabilities: Building Layers of Competitive Advantage   19

a. Thomas J. Peters
b. Abraham Harold Maslow
c. Adam Smith
d. Affiliation

8. Procter is a surname, and may also refer to:

   - Bryan Waller Procter (pseud. Barry Cornwall), English poet
   - Goodwin Procter, American law firm
   - _____, consumer products multinational

a. Master and Servant Acts
b. Downstream
c. Procter ' Gamble
d. Strict liability

9. _____ as defined in business terms is an organization's strategic guide to globalization. A sound _____ should address these questions: what must be (versus what is) the extent of market presence in the world's major markets? How to build the necessary global presence? What must be (versus what is) the optimal locations around the world for the various value chain activities? How to run global presence into global competitive advantage?

Academic research on _____ came of age during the 1980s, including work by Michael Porter and Christopher Bartlett ' Sumantra Ghoshal. Among the forces perceived to bring about the globalization of competition were convergence in economic systems and technological change, especially in information technology, that facilitated and required the coordination of a multinational firm's strategy on a worldwide scale.

a. 28-hour day
b. 33 Strategies of War
c. 1990 Clean Air Act
d. Global strategy

10. _____ has been described as the 'process of social influence in which one person can enlist the aid and support of others in the accomplishment of a common task' . A definition more inclusive of followers comes from Alan Keith of Genentech who said '_____ is ultimately about creating a way for people to contribute to making something extraordinary happen.'

_____ is one of the most salient aspects of the organizational context. However, defining _____ has been challenging.

Chapter 3. Developing Strategic Capabilities: Building Layers of Competitive Advantage

a. Leadership
b. Situational leadership
c. 28-hour day
d. 1990 Clean Air Act

11. _____ is an integrated communications-based process through which individuals and communities discover that existing and newly-identified needs and wants may be satisfied by the products and services of others.

_____ is defined by the American _____ Association as the activity, set of institutions, and processes for creating, communicating, delivering, and exchanging offerings that have value for customers, clients, partners, and society at large. The term developed from the original meaning which referred literally to going to market, as in shopping, or going to a market to buy or sell goods or services.

a. Disruptive technology
b. Market development
c. Customer relationship management
d. Marketing

12. In business and engineering, new _____ is the term used to describe the complete process of bringing a new product or service to market. There are two parallel paths involved in the NProduct development process: one involves the idea generation, product design, and detail engineering; the other involves market research and marketing analysis. Companies typically see new _____ as the first stage in generating and commercializing new products within the overall strategic process of product life cycle management used to maintain or grow their market share.
a. 33 Strategies of War
b. 28-hour day
c. 1990 Clean Air Act
d. Product development

13. _____ is one of the four Ps of the marketing mix. The other three aspects are product, promotion, and place. It is also a key variable in microeconomic price allocation theory.
a. Transfer pricing
b. Pricing
c. Price floor
d. Penetration pricing

14. The term '_____' refers to the concept of collecting information and attempting to spot a pattern in the information. In some fields of study, the term '_____' has more formally-defined meanings.

In project management _____ is a mathematical technique that uses historical results to predict future outcome.

a. Regression analysis
b. Least squares
c. Stepwise regression
d. Trend analysis

15. _____ can be defined as the idea generation, concept development, testing and manufacturing or implementation of a physical object or service. _____ers conceptualize and evaluate ideas, making them tangible through products in a more systematic approach. The role of a _____er encompasses many characteristics of the marketing manager, product manager, industrial designer and design engineer.
   a. Adam Smith
   b. Product design
   c. Abraham Harold Maslow
   d. Affiliation

16. _____ is an increasingly broadening term with which an organization, or other human system describes the combination of traditionally administrative personnel functions with acquisition and application of skills, knowledge and experience, Employee Relations and resource planning at various levels. The field draws upon concepts developed in Industrial/Organizational Psychology and System Theory. _____ has at least two related interpretations depending on context. The original usage derives from political economy and economics, where it was traditionally called labor, one of four factors of production although this perspective is changing as a function of new and ongoing research into more strategic approaches at national levels. This first usage is used more in terms of '_____ development', and can go beyond just organizations to the level of nations . The more traditional usage within corporations and businesses refers to the individuals within a firm or agency, and to the portion of the organization that deals with hiring, firing, training, and other personnel issues, typically referred to as `_____ management'.
   a. Progressive discipline
   b. Bradford Factor
   c. Human resource management
   d. Human resources

17. The phrase mergers and _____s refers to the aspect of corporate strategy, corporate finance and management dealing with the buying, selling and combining of different companies that can aid, finance, or help a growing company in a given industry grow rapidly without having to create another business entity.

An _____, also known as a takeover or a buyout, is the buying of one company (the 'target') by another. An _____ may be friendly or hostile.

22 *Chapter 3. Developing Strategic Capabilities: Building Layers of Competitive Advantage*

a. A4e
b. AAAI
c. A Stake in the Outcome
d. Acquisition

18. _____ in its literal sense is the process of transformation of local or regional phenomena into global ones. It can be described as a process by which the people of the world are unified into a single society and function together.

This process is a combination of economic, technological, sociocultural and political forces.

a. Histogram
b. Globalization
c. Collaborative Planning, Forecasting and Replenishment
d. Cost Management

19. A _____ or transnational corporation is a corporation or enterprise that manages production or delivers services in more than one country. It can also be referred to as an international corporation.

The first modern _____ is generally thought to be the Dutch East India Company, established in 1602.

a. Small and medium enterprises
b. Financial Accounting Standards Board
c. Command center
d. Multinational corporation

20. _____ is a term used to describe policies which emphasize on domestic control of the economy, labor and capital formation, even if this requires the imposition of tariffs and other restrictions on the movement of labour, goods and capital. It is in opposition to globalization in many cases, or at least it questions the benefits of unrestricted free trade. _____ may include such doctrines as protectionism and import substitution.

a. A Stake in the Outcome
b. AAAI
c. A4e
d. Economic nationalism

Chapter 3. Developing Strategic Capabilities: Building Layers of Competitive Advantage

21. _____ was a writer, management consultant, and self-described 'social ecologist.' Widely considered to be 'the father of modern management,' his 39 books and countless scholarly and popular articles explored how humans are organized across all sectors of society--in business, government and the nonprofit world. His writings have predicted many of the major developments of the late twentieth century, including privatization and decentralization; the rise of Japan to economic world power; the decisive importance of marketing; and the emergence of the information society with its necessity of lifelong learning. In 1959, Drucker coined the term 'knowledge worker' and later in his life considered knowledge work productivity to be the next frontier of management.
   a. Chrissie Hynde
   b. Jacques Al-Salawat Nasruddin Nasser
   c. Debora L. Spar
   d. Peter Ferdinand Drucker

22. _____ refers to the difference between the cost of materials purchased by a company plus the cost of the labor to assemble a product and the price at which the company sells the product. An example is the price of gasoline at the pump over the price of the oil in it. In national accounts used in macroeconomics, it refers to the contribution of the factors of production, i.e., land, labor, and capital goods, to raising the value of a product and corresponds to the incomes received by the owners of these factors.
   a. Minimum wage
   b. Rehn-Meidner Model
   c. Deregulation
   d. Value added

23. _____ is a concept related to the relative abilities of parties in a situation to exert influence over each other. If both parties are on an equal footing in a debate, then they will have equal _____, such as in a perfectly competitive market, or between an evenly matched monopoly and monopsony.

There are a number of fields where the concept of _____ has proven crucial to coherent analysis: game theory, labour economics, collective bargaining arrangements, diplomatic negotiations, settlement of litigation, the price of insurance, and any negotiation in general.

   a. Trade credit
   b. Buy-sell agreement
   c. 1990 Clean Air Act
   d. Bargaining power

24. In economics, business, retail, and accounting, a _____ is the value of money that has been used up to produce something, and hence is not available for use anymore. In economics, a _____ is an alternative that is given up as a result of a decision. In business, the _____ may be one of acquisition, in which case the amount of money expended to acquire it is counted as _____.

Chapter 3. Developing Strategic Capabilities: Building Layers of Competitive Advantage

   a. Cost
   b. Cost overrun
   c. Fixed costs
   d. Cost allocation

25. _____ is the management of the flow of goods, information and other resources, including energy and people, between the point of origin and the point of consumption in order to meet the requirements of consumers (frequently, and originally, military organizations.) _____ involves the integration of information, transportation, inventory, warehousing, material-handling, and packaging, and occasionally security. _____ is a channel of the supply chain which adds the value of time and place utility.
   a. 1990 Clean Air Act
   b. Logistics
   c. Third-party logistics
   d. 28-hour day

26. In business, the term word _____ refers to a number of procurement practices, aimed at finding, evaluating and engaging suppliers of goods and services:

- Global _____, a procurement strategy aimed at exploiting global efficiencies in production
- Strategic _____, a component of supply chain management, for improving and re-evaluating purchasing activities
- _____, the identification of job candidates through proactive recruiting technique
- Co-_____, a type of auditing service
- Low-cost country _____, a procurement strategy for acquiring materials from countries with lower labour and production costs in order to cut operating expenses
- Corporate _____, a supply chain, purchasing/procurement, and inventory function
- Second-tier _____, a practice of rewarding suppliers for attempting to achieve minority-owned business spending goals of their customer
- Netsourcing, a practice of utilizing an established group of businesses, individuals, or hardware ' software applications to streamline or initiate procurement practices by tapping in to and working through a third party provider
- Inverted _____, a price volatility reduction strategy usually conducted by procurement or supply-chain person by which the value of an organization's waste-stream is maximized by actively seeking out the highest price possible from a range of potential buyers exploiting price trends and other market factors
- Multisourcing, a strategy that treats a given function, such as IT, as a portfolio of activities, some of which should be outsourced and others of which should be performed by internal staff.
- Crowdsourcing, using an undefined, generally large group of people or community in the form of an open call to perform a task

Chapter 3. Developing Strategic Capabilities: Building Layers of Competitive Advantage

In journalism, it can also refer to:

- Journalism _____, the practice of identifying a person or publication that gives information
- Single _____, the reuse of content in publishing

In computing, it can refer to:

- Open-_____, the act of releasing previously proprietary software under an open source/free software license
- Power _____ equipment, network devices that will provide power in a Power over Ethernet (PoE) setup

a. Continuous
b. Reinforcement
c. Cost Management
d. Sourcing

27. _____ is a dynamic of being mutually and physically responsible to and sharing a common set of principles with others. This concept differs distinctly from 'dependence' in that an interdependent relationship implies that all participants are emotionally, economically, ecologically and or morally 'interdependent.' Some people advocate freedom or independence as a sort of ultimate good; others do the same with devotion to one's family, community, or society. _____ recognizes the truth in each position and weaves them together.
a. A Stake in the Outcome
b. A4e
c. Interdependence
d. AAAI

28. A _____ is an established norm or requirement. It is usually a formal document that establishes uniform engineering or technical criteria, methods, processes and practices.

A _____ can also be a controlled artifact or similar formal means used for calibration.

a. 28-hour day
b. 1990 Clean Air Act
c. 33 Strategies of War
d. Technical standard

Chapter 3. Developing Strategic Capabilities: Building Layers of Competitive Advantage

29. The _____ is a concept from business management that was first described and popularized by Michael Porter in his 1985 best-seller, Competitive Advantage: Creating and Sustaining Superior Performance.

A _____ is a chain of activities. Products pass through all activities of the chain in order and at each activity the product gains some value. The chain of activities gives the products more added value than the sum of added values of all activities. It is important not to mix the concept of the _____ with the costs occurring throughout the activities.

   a. Value chain
   b. Customer relationship management
   c. Mass marketing
   d. Market development

30. _____ is the acquisition of goods and/or services at the best possible total cost of ownership, in the right quality and quantity, at the right time, in the right place and from the right source for the direct benefit or use of corporations, individuals generally via a contract. Simple _____ may involve nothing more than repeat purchasing. Complex _____ could involve finding long term partners - or even 'co-destiny' suppliers that might fundamentally commit one organization to another.
   a. Psychological pricing
   b. Golden parachute
   c. Sole proprietorship
   d. Procurement

31. _____ is one of the managerial functions like planning, organizing, staffing and directing. It is an important function because it helps to check the errors and to take the corrective action so that deviation from standards are minimized and stated goals of the organization are achieved in desired manner. According to modern concepts, _____ is a foreseeing action whereas earlier concept of _____ was used only when errors were detected. _____ in management means setting standards, measuring actual performance and taking corrective action.
   a. Turnover
   b. Schedule of reinforcement
   c. Control
   d. Decision tree pruning

32. In economics, _____ refers to the ability of a person or a country to produce a particular good at a lower marginal cost and opportunity cost than another person or country. It is the ability to produce a product most efficiently given all the other products that could be produced. It can be contrasted with absolute advantage which refers to the ability of a person or a country to produce a particular good at a lower absolute cost than another.

Chapter 3. Developing Strategic Capabilities: Building Layers of Competitive Advantage 27

   a. 33 Strategies of War
   b. 28-hour day
   c. 1990 Clean Air Act
   d. Comparative advantage

33. _____ is the advantage gained by the initial occupant of a market segment. This advantage may stem from the fact that the first entrant can gain control of resources that followers may not be able to match. Sometimes the first mover is not able to capitalise on its advantage, leaving the opportunity for another firm to gain second-mover advantage.
   a. First-mover advantage
   b. Business ecosystem
   c. Customer retention
   d. Horizontal integration

34. _____ is a concept developed by Michael Porter, used in business strategy. It describes a way to establish the competitive advantage. _____, in basic words, means the lowest cost of operation in the industry.
   a. Switching cost
   b. Strategic group
   c. Strategic business unit
   d. Cost leadership

Chapter 4. Developing Coordination and Control: The Organizational Challenge

1. _____ is one of the managerial functions like planning, organizing, staffing and directing. It is an important function because it helps to check the errors and to take the corrective action so that deviation from standards are minimized and stated goals of the organization are achieved in desired manner.According to modern concepts, _____ is a foreseeing action whereas earlier concept of _____ was used only when errors were detected. _____ in management means setting standards, measuring actual performance and taking corrective action.
    a. Decision tree pruning
    b. Control
    c. Turnover
    d. Schedule of reinforcement

2. A _____ or transnational corporation is a corporation or enterprise that manages production or delivers services in more than one country. It can also be referred to as an international corporation.

    The first modern _____ is generally thought to be the Dutch East India Company, established in 1602.

    a. Financial Accounting Standards Board
    b. Small and medium enterprises
    c. Command center
    d. Multinational corporation

3. _____ is the process by which the activities of an organisation, particularly those regarding decision-making, become concentrated within a particular location and/or group.
    a. Centralization
    b. Product innovation
    c. Chief operating officer
    d. Corner office

4. Procter is a surname, and may also refer to:

    - Bryan Waller Procter (pseud. Barry Cornwall), English poet
    - Goodwin Procter, American law firm
    - _____, consumer products multinational

    a. Downstream
    b. Strict liability
    c. Master and Servant Acts
    d. Procter ' Gamble

Chapter 4. Developing Coordination and Control: The Organizational Challenge

5. _____ is the most common type of organizational management. The organization is grouped by areas of specialty within different functional areas (e.g., finance, marketing, and engineering.) Some refer to a functional area as a 'silo.' Communication generally occurs within a single department.
   a. Micromanagement
   b. Distributed Development
   c. Functional management
   d. Workflow

6. As defined by Richard Beckhard, _____ is a planned, top-down, organization-wide effort to increase the organization's effectiveness and health. _____ is achieved through interventions in the organization's 'processes,' using behavioural science knowledge. According to Warren Bennis, _____ is a complex strategy intended to change the beliefs, attitudes, values, and structure of organizations so that they can better adapt to new technologies, markets, and challenges.
   a. Organizational structure
   b. Organizational culture
   c. Organizational development
   d. Informal organization

7. _____ is the corporate management term for the act of reorganizing the legal, ownership, operational, or other structures of a company for the purpose of making it more profitable, or better organized for its present needs. Alternate reasons for _____ include a change of ownership or ownership structure, demerger repositioning debt _____ and financial _____.
   a. Market value added
   b. Restructuring
   c. Market value
   d. Net worth

8. In neuroscience, the _____ is a collection of brain structures which attempts to regulate and control behavior by inducing pleasurable effects.

A psychological reward is a process that reinforces behavior -- something that, when offered, causes a behavior to increase in intensity. Reward is an operational concept for describing the positive value an individual ascribes to an object, behavioral act or an internal physical state.

   a. 1990 Clean Air Act
   b. 33 Strategies of War
   c. 28-hour day
   d. Reward system

9. A _____ is directly responsible for managing the day-to-day operations (and profitability) of a company.

Chief Executive Officer (CEO)
- As the top manager, the CEO is typically responsible for the entire operations of the corporation and reports directly to the chairman and board of directors. It is the CEO's responsibility to implement board decisions and initiatives and to maintain the smooth operation of the firm, with the assistance of senior management.

   a. Vorstand
   b. Field service management
   c. Getting Things Done
   d. Management team

10. An _____ is a mostly hierarchical concept of subordination of entities that collaborate and contribute to serve one common aim.

Organizations are a variant of clustered entities. The structure of an organization is usually set up in many a styles, dependent on their objectives and ambience.

   a. Organizational development
   b. Informal organization
   c. Open shop
   d. Organizational structure

11. _____ is the principle that the government must respect all of the legal rights that are owed to a person according to the law of the land. As developed through a large body of case law in the United States, this principle gives individuals a varying ability to enforce their rights against alleged violations by governments and their agents (that is, state actors), but normally not against other private citizens.

_____ has also been frequently interpreted as placing limitations on laws and legal proceedings, in order for judges instead of legislators to define and guarantee fundamental fairness, justice, and liberty.

   a. Maximum medical improvement
   b. Clayton Antitrust Act
   c. Sick leave
   d. Due process

Chapter 4. Developing Coordination and Control: The Organizational Challenge

12. _____ is the act by an employer of terminating employment. Though such a decision can be made by an employer for a variety of reasons, ranging from an economic downturn to performance-related problems on the part of the employee, being fired has a strong stigma in many cultures. To be fired, as opposed to quitting voluntarily (or being laid off), is often perceived as being the employee's fault, and is therefore considered to be disgraceful and a sign of failure.

   a. Termination of employment
   b. Severance package
   c. Layoff
   d. Firing

13. _____ in Public Relations

There are different types of _____ in public relations; symmetric and asymmetric.

Two-way asymmetric public relations...>· can also be called 'scientific persuasion;'>· employs social science methods to develop more persuasive communication;>· generally focuses on achieving short-term attitude change;>· incorporates lots of feedback from target audiences and publics;>· is used by an organization primarily interested in having its publics come around to its way of thinking rather changing the organization, its policies, or its views.

Two-way symmetric public relations...>· relies on honest and open _____ and mutual give-and-take rather than one-way persuasion;>· focuses on mutual respect and efforts to achieve mutual understanding;>· emphasizes negotiation and a willingness to adapt and make compromises;>· requires organizations engaging in public relations to be willing to make significant adjustments in how they operate in order to accommodate their publics;>· seems to be used more by non-profit organizations, government agencies, and heavily regulated businesses such as public utilities than by competitive, profit-driven companies.

   a. Public relations
   b. 28-hour day
   c. Two-way communication
   d. 1990 Clean Air Act

14. _____ as defined in business terms is an organization's strategic guide to globalization. A sound _____ should address these questions: what must be (versus what is) the extent of market presence in the world's major markets? How to build the necessary global presence? What must be (versus what is) the optimal locations around the world for the various value chain activities? How to run global presence into global competitive advantage?

Academic research on _____ came of age during the 1980s, including work by Michael Porter and Christopher Bartlett ' Sumantra Ghoshal. Among the forces perceived to bring about the globalization of competition were convergence in economic systems and technological change, especially in information technology, that facilitated and required the coordination of a multinational firm's strategy on a worldwide scale.

a. 1990 Clean Air Act
b. 28-hour day
c. 33 Strategies of War
d. Global strategy

15. In economics and game theory, _____ are games of incomplete information where players receive possibly-correlated signals of the underlying state of the world. _____ were originally defined by Carlsson and van Damme (1993.) The most important practical application of _____ has been the study of crises in financial markets such as bank runs, currency crises, and bubbles .
a. Perfect information
b. Mixed strategy
c. Transferable utility
d. Global games

16. _____ is a British telecommunications company. In the mid-1980s, it became the first company in the UK to offer an alternative telephone service to British Telecom (via subsidiary Mercury Communications, merged into C'W in 1997.)
a. Drummond Company
b. Merck ' Co., Inc.
c. Global Trade Watch
d. Cable ' Wireless

17. _____ is an integrated communications-based process through which individuals and communities discover that existing and newly-identified needs and wants may be satisfied by the products and services of others.

_____ is defined by the American _____ Association as the activity, set of institutions, and processes for creating, communicating, delivering, and exchanging offerings that have value for customers, clients, partners, and society at large. The term developed from the original meaning which referred literally to going to market, as in shopping, or going to a market to buy or sell goods or services.

a. Market development
b. Disruptive technology
c. Customer relationship management
d. Marketing

Chapter 4. Developing Coordination and Control: The Organizational Challenge

18. In economics and sociology, an _____ is any factor (financial or non-financial) that enables or motivates a particular course of action, or counts as a reason for preferring one choice to the alternatives. It is an expectation that encourages people to behave in a certain way. Since human beings are purposeful creatures, the study of _____ structures is central to the study of all economic activity (both in terms of individual decision-making and in terms of co-operation and competition within a larger institutional structure.)
    a. Incentive
    b. AAAI
    c. A4e
    d. A Stake in the Outcome

34 *Chapter 5. Creating and Leveraging Knowledge: The Worldwide Learning Challenge*

1. Procter is a surname, and may also refer to:

   - Bryan Waller Procter (pseud. Barry Cornwall), English poet
   - Goodwin Procter, American law firm
   - _____, consumer products multinational

   a. Master and Servant Acts
   b. Strict liability
   c. Procter ' Gamble
   d. Downstream

2. _____ of the learning curve effect and the closely related experience curve effect express the relationship between equations for experience and efficiency or between efficiency gains and investment in the effort. The experience of 'learning curves' was first observed by the 19th Century German psychologist Hermann Ebbinghaus according to the difficulty of memorizing varying numbers of verbal stimuli, and subsequent learning about the complex processes of learning are discussed in the

   The rule used for representing the learning curve effect states that the more times a task has been performed, the less time will be required on each subsequent iteration.

   a. Distribution
   b. Point biserial correlation coefficient
   c. Spatial Decision Support Systems
   d. Models

3. A _____, in business matters, is an entity that is controlled by a bigger and more powerful entity. The controlled entity is called a company, corporation, or limited liability company and in some cases can be a government or state-owned enterprise, and the controlling entity is called its parent (or the parent company.) The reason for this distinction is that a lone company cannot be a _____ of any organization; only an entity representing a legal fiction as a separate entity can be a _____.

   a. 1990 Clean Air Act
   b. 33 Strategies of War
   c. 28-hour day
   d. Subsidiary

Chapter 5. Creating and Leveraging Knowledge: The Worldwide Learning Challenge

4. A _____ is a list of the general tasks and responsibilities of a position. Typically, it also includes to whom the position reports, specifications such as the qualifications needed by the person in the job, salary range for the position, etc. A _____ is usually developed by conducting a job analysis, which includes examining the tasks and sequences of tasks necessary to perform the job.

   a. Recruitment
   b. Recruitment advertising
   c. Recruitment Process Insourcing
   d. Job description

5. _____ is a dynamic of being mutually and physically responsible to and sharing a common set of principles with others. This concept differs distinctly from 'dependence' in that an interdependent relationship implies that all participants are emotionally, economically, ecologically and or morally 'interdependent.' Some people advocate freedom or independence as a sort of ultimate good; others do the same with devotion to one's family, community, or society. _____ recognizes the truth in each position and weaves them together.

   a. Interdependence
   b. A Stake in the Outcome
   c. AAAI
   d. A4e

6. _____ is the self-government of a nation, country or some portion thereof, generally exercising sovereignty.

   The term _____ is used in contrast to subjugation, which refers to a region as a 'territory' --subject to the political and military control of an external government. The word is sometimes used in a weaker sense to contrast with hegemony, the indirect control of one nation by another, more powerful nation.

   a. A4e
   b. A Stake in the Outcome
   c. AAAI
   d. Independence

7. The _____ of an edge is $c_f(u,v) = c(u,v) - f(u,v)$. This defines a residual network denoted $G_f(V, \overline{E_f})$, giving the amount of available capacity. See that there can be an edge from u to v in the residual network, even though there is no edge from u to v in the original network.

   a. 33 Strategies of War
   b. 28-hour day
   c. 1990 Clean Air Act
   d. Residual capacity

Chapter 5. Creating and Leveraging Knowledge: The Worldwide Learning Challenge

8. _____ is one of the managerial functions like planning, organizing, staffing and directing. It is an important function because it helps to check the errors and to take the corrective action so that deviation from standards are minimized and stated goals of the organization are achieved in desired manner. According to modern concepts, _____ is a foreseeing action whereas earlier concept of _____ was used only when errors were detected. _____ in management means setting standards, measuring actual performance and taking corrective action.
   a. Turnover
   b. Decision tree pruning
   c. Schedule of reinforcement
   d. Control

9. _____ is the process by which the activities of an organisation, particularly those regarding decision-making, become concentrated within a particular location and/or group.
   a. Centralization
   b. Product innovation
   c. Corner office
   d. Chief operating officer

10. In economics and game theory, _____ are games of incomplete information where players receive possibly-correlated signals of the underlying state of the world. _____ were originally defined by Carlsson and van Damme (1993.) The most important practical application of _____ has been the study of crises in financial markets such as bank runs, currency crises, and bubbles.
    a. Transferable utility
    b. Mixed strategy
    c. Perfect information
    d. Global games

11. _____ is a worldwide management consulting firm that focuses on solving issues of concern to senior management. McKinsey serves as an advisor to the world's leading businesses, governments, and institutions. It is widely recognized as a leader and one of the most prestigious firms in the management consulting industry.
    a. 28-hour day
    b. 1990 Clean Air Act
    c. 33 Strategies of War
    d. McKinsey ' Company

12. _____ comprises a range of practices used in an organisation to identify, create, represent, distribute and enable adoption of insights and experiences. Such insights and experiences comprise knowledge, either embodied in individuals or embedded in organisational processes or practice.

Chapter 5. Creating and Leveraging Knowledge: The Worldwide Learning Challenge 37

An established discipline since 1991 , _____ includes courses taught in the fields of business administration, information systems, management, and library and information sciences .

a. 1990 Clean Air Act
b. 28-hour day
c. 33 Strategies of War
d. Knowledge management

13. _____ is an organization's process of defining its strategy and making decisions on allocating its resources to pursue this strategy, including its capital and people. Various business analysis techniques can be used in _____, including SWOT analysis (Strengths, Weaknesses, Opportunities, and Threats) and PEST analysis (Political, Economic, Social, and Technological analysis) or STEER analysis involving Socio-cultural, Technological, Economic, Ecological, and Regulatory factors and EPISTEL (Environment, Political, Informatic, Social, Technological, Economic and Legal)

_____ is the formal consideration of an organization's future course. All _____ deals with at least one of three key questions:

1. 'What do we do?'
2. 'For whom do we do it?'
3. 'How do we excel?'

In business _____, the third question is better phrased 'How can we beat or avoid competition?'. (Bradford and Duncan, page 1.)

a. Strategic planning
b. 33 Strategies of War
c. 1990 Clean Air Act
d. 28-hour day

14. A _____ is a framework for creating economic, social, and/or other forms of value. The term _____ is thus used for a broad range of informal and formal descriptions to represent core aspects of a business, including purpose, offerings, strategies, infrastructure, organizational structures, trading practices, and operational processes and policies.

Conceptualizations of _____s try to formalize informal descriptions into building blocks and their relationships.

Chapter 5. Creating and Leveraging Knowledge: The Worldwide Learning Challenge

a. Gap analysis
b. Business model design
c. Business networking
d. Business model

15. _____ is the process of sharing of skills, knowledge, technologies, methods of manufacturing, samples of manufacturing and facilities among governments and other institutions to ensure that scientific and technological developments are accessible to a wider range of users who can then further develop and exploit the technology into new products, processes, applications, materials or services. It is closely related to (and may arguably be considered a subset of) Knowledge transfer. Related terms, used almost synonymously, include 'technology valorisation' and 'technology commercialisation'.

a. Munn v. Illinois
b. Mediation
c. Competition law
d. Technology transfer

16. In general, _____ consists of expansionist policies of government. While some have linked the term to promoting economic growth (in contrast to no growth / sustainable policies), more commonly _____ refers to the doctrine of a nation's expanding its territorial base (or economic influence) usually by means of military aggression. Compare empire-building and Lebensraum.

a. A4e
b. A Stake in the Outcome
c. Expansionism
d. AAAI

17. A _____ or transnational corporation is a corporation or enterprise that manages production or delivers services in more than one country. It can also be referred to as an international corporation.

The first modern _____ is generally thought to be the Dutch East India Company, established in 1602.

a. Financial Accounting Standards Board
b. Multinational corporation
c. Command center
d. Small and medium enterprises

Chapter 5. Creating and Leveraging Knowledge: The Worldwide Learning Challenge

18. A _____ is a type of business entity in which partners (owners) share with each other the profits or losses of the business. _____s are often favored over corporations for taxation purposes, as the _____ structure does not generally incur a tax on profits before it is distributed to the partners (i.e. there is no dividend tax levied.) However, depending on the _____ structure and the jurisdiction in which it operates, owners of a _____ may be exposed to greater personal liability than they would as shareholders of a corporation.
    a. Due process
    b. Mediation
    c. Partnership
    d. Federal Employers Liability Act

19. A _____ is an invitation for suppliers, often through a bidding process, to submit a proposal on a specific commodity or service. A bidding process is one of the best methods for leveraging a company's negotiating ability and purchasing power with suppliers. The _____ process brings structure to the procurement decision and allows the risks and benefits to be identified clearly upfront.
    a. 1990 Clean Air Act
    b. Request for proposal
    c. Lead generation
    d. Lead management

20. _____ is a term used to describe persistent social, corporate or institutional culture that avoids using or buying already existing products, research or knowledge because of its different origins. It is normally used in a pejorative sense.

    As a social phenomenon, '_____' syndrome is manifested as an unwillingness to adopt an idea or product because it originates from another culture, a form of nationalism.

    a. 1990 Clean Air Act
    b. 28-hour day
    c. 33 Strategies of War
    d. Not Invented Here

21. In microeconomics and strategic management, the term _____ describes a type of ownership and control. It is a strategy used by a business or corporation that seeks to sell a type of product in numerous markets. _____ in marketing is much more common than vertical integration is in production.
    a. Horizontal integration
    b. Farmshoring
    c. No-bid contract
    d. Career development

Chapter 5. Creating and Leveraging Knowledge: The Worldwide Learning Challenge

22. _____, widely known as F. W. Taylor, was an American mechanical engineer who sought to improve industrial efficiency. He is regarded as the father of scientific management, and was one of the first management consultants.

Taylor was one of the intellectual leaders of the Efficiency Movement and his ideas, broadly conceived, were highly influential in the Progressive Era.

a. Frederick Winslow Taylor
b. Geoffrey Colvin
c. Douglas N. Daft
d. Jonah Jacob Goldberg

23. _____ is the current President of Barnard College, a liberal arts college for women affiliated with Columbia University; as President of Barnard, she is also an academic dean within the university. Spar became Barnard's 11th president in 2008 after a teaching career at Harvard Business School where she was Senior Associate Dean for Faculty Research and Development. After graduating magna cum laude from the Georgetown University School of Foreign Service and earning her doctorate from Harvard in government, she went on to write 6 books and many articles.

a. John Jacob Astor
b. Bruce Edward Babbitt
c. Debora L. Spar
d. Carol Ann Bartz

Chapter 6. Managing across Boundaries: The Collaborative Challenge   41

1. A _____ is an entity formed between two or more parties to undertake economic activity together. The parties agree to create a new entity by both contributing equity, and they then share in the revenues, expenses, and control of the enterprise. The venture can be for one specific project only, or a continuing business relationship such as the Fuji Xerox _____.
   a. Patent
   b. Joint venture
   c. Meritor Savings Bank v. Vinson
   d. Civil Rights Act of 1991

2. A _____ is a formal relationship between two or more parties to pursue a set of agreed upon goals or to meet a critical business need while remaining independent organizations.

   Partners may provide the _____ with resources such as products, distribution channels, manufacturing capability, project funding, capital equipment, knowledge, expertise, or intellectual property. The alliance is a cooperation or collaboration which aims for a synergy where each partner hopes that the benefits from the alliance will be greater than those from individual efforts.

   a. Golden parachute
   b. Process automation
   c. Farmshoring
   d. Strategic Alliance

3. An _____ is a person who has possession of an enterprise and assumes significant accountability for the inherent risks and the outcome. It is an ambitious leader who combines land, labor, and capital to create and market new goods or services. The term is a loanword from French and was first defined by the Irish economist Richard Cantillon.
   a. A Stake in the Outcome
   b. AAAI
   c. Entrepreneur
   d. A4e

4. _____, in microeconomics, are the cost advantages that a business obtains due to expansion. They are factors that cause a producer's average cost per unit to fall as scale is increased. _____ is a long run concept and refers to reductions in unit cost as the size of a facility, or scale, increases.
   a. A4e
   b. Economies of scope
   c. A Stake in the Outcome
   d. Economies of scale

5. In decision theory and estimation theory, the _____ of an estimator, $\hat{\theta}$, of an unknown parameter of the distribution, θ, is the expected value of the loss function

$$R(\theta, \hat{\theta}) = \mathbb{E}_\theta L(\theta, \hat{\theta}) = \int L(\theta, \hat{\theta})\, dP_\theta.$$

where dP_θ is a probability measure parametrized by θ.

- For a scalar parameter θ and a quadratic loss function,

$$L(\theta, \hat{\theta}) = (\theta - \hat{\theta})^2$$

the _____ function becomes the mean squared error of the estimate,

$$R(\theta, \hat{\theta}) = E_\theta(\theta - \hat{\theta})^2$$

- In density estimation, the unknown parameter is probability density itself. The loss function is typically chosen to be a norm in an appropriate function space. For example, for L^2 norm,

$$L(f, \hat{f}) = \|f - \hat{f}\|_2^2$$

the _____ function becomes the mean integrated squared error

$$R(f, \hat{f}) = E\|f - \hat{f}\|^2$$

a. Financial modeling
b. Risk aversion
c. Linear model
d. Risk

6. In economics, business, retail, and accounting, a _____ is the value of money that has been used up to produce something, and hence is not available for use anymore. In economics, a _____ is an alternative that is given up as a result of a decision. In business, the _____ may be one of acquisition, in which case the amount of money expended to acquire it is counted as _____.

Chapter 6. Managing across Boundaries: The Collaborative Challenge

a. Cost overrun
b. Fixed costs
c. Cost allocation
d. Cost

7. The _____ of an edge is $c_f(u, v) = c(u, v) - f(u, v)$. This defines a residual network denoted $G_f(V, \overline{E_f})$, giving the amount of available capacity. See that there can be an edge from u to v in the residual network, even though there is no edge from u to v in the original network.

a. 28-hour day
b. 33 Strategies of War
c. 1990 Clean Air Act
d. Residual capacity

8. _____ is an organization's process of defining its strategy and making decisions on allocating its resources to pursue this strategy, including its capital and people. Various business analysis techniques can be used in _____, including SWOT analysis (Strengths, Weaknesses, Opportunities, and Threats) and PEST analysis (Political, Economic, Social, and Technological analysis) or STEER analysis involving Socio-cultural, Technological, Economic, Ecological, and Regulatory factors and EPISTEL (Environment, Political, Informatic, Social, Technological, Economic and Legal)

_____ is the formal consideration of an organization's future course. All _____ deals with at least one of three key questions:

1. 'What do we do?'
2. 'For whom do we do it?'
3. 'How do we excel?'

In business _____, the third question is better phrased 'How can we beat or avoid competition?'. (Bradford and Duncan, page 1.)

a. Strategic planning
b. 33 Strategies of War
c. 28-hour day
d. 1990 Clean Air Act

9. In finance, an _____ is a contract between a buyer and a seller that gives the buyer the right--but not the obligation-- to buy or to sell a particular asset (the underlying asset) at a later day at an agreed price. In return for granting the _____, the seller collects a payment (the premium) from the buyer. A call _____ gives the buyer the right to buy the underlying asset; a put _____ gives the buyer of the _____ the right to sell the underlying asset.

a. A Stake in the Outcome
b. AAAI
c. A4e
d. Option

10. In business and engineering, new _____ is the term used to describe the complete process of bringing a new product or service to market. There are two parallel paths involved in the NProduct development process: one involves the idea generation, product design, and detail engineering; the other involves market research and marketing analysis. Companies typically see new _____ as the first stage in generating and commercializing new products within the overall strategic process of product life cycle management used to maintain or grow their market share.
a. 1990 Clean Air Act
b. 28-hour day
c. 33 Strategies of War
d. Product development

11. The _____ (Situation, Task, Action, Result) format is a job interview technique used by interviewers to gather all the relevant information about a specific capability that the job requires. This interview format is said to have a higher degree of predictability of future on-the-job performance than the traditional interview.

- Situation: The interviewer wants you to present a recent challenge and situation in which you found yourself.
- Task: What did you have to achieve? The interviewer will be looking to see what you were trying to achieve from the situation.
- Action: What did you do? The interviewer will be looking for information on what you did, why you did it and what were the alternatives.
- Results: What was the outcome of your actions? What did you achieve through your actions and did you meet your objectives. What did you learn from this experience and have you used this learning since?

a. Competency-based job descriptions
b. Rasch models
c. Phrase completion
d. Star

12. _____ is the removal or simplification of government rules and regulations that constrain the operation of market forces. _____ does not mean elimination of laws against fraud, but eliminating or reducing government control of how business is done, thereby moving toward a more free market.

The stated rationale for '_____' is often that fewer and simpler regulations will lead to a raised level of competitiveness, therefore higher productivity, more efficiency and lower prices overall.

Chapter 6. Managing across Boundaries: The Collaborative Challenge 45

a. Value added
b. Rehn-Meidner Model
c. Deregulation
d. Natural rate of unemployment

13. _____ generally refers to a list of all planned expenses and revenues. It is a plan for saving and spending. A _____ is an important concept in microeconomics, which uses a _____ line to illustrate the trade-offs between two or more goods.

a. 1990 Clean Air Act
b. Budget
c. 33 Strategies of War
d. 28-hour day

14. _____ is a civil designation for persons who are incorporated in a fixed or permanent way to a society or group: regular member of the working staff, permanent staff distinguished from a supernumerary.

The term '_____' and its counterpart, 'supernumerary,' originated in Spanish and Latin American academy and government; it is now also used in countries all over the world, such as France, the U.S., England, Italy, etc.

There are _____ members of surgical organizations, of universities, of gastronomical associations, etc.

a. Numerary
b. Affiliation
c. Abraham Harold Maslow
d. Adam Smith

15. In marketing, _____ has come to mean the process by which marketers try to create an image or identity in the minds of their target market for its product, brand, or organization. It is the 'relative competitive comparison' their product occupies in a given market as perceived by the target market.

Re-_____ involves changing the identity of a product, relative to the identity of competing products, in the collective minds of the target market.

a. Context analysis
b. Customer analytics
c. PEST analysis
d. Positioning

16. In economics, _____ are business expenses that are not dependent on the activities of the business They tend to be time-related, such as salaries or rents being paid per month. This is in contrast to variable costs, which are volume-related (and are paid per quantity.)

In management accounting, _____ are defined as expenses that do not change in proportion to the activity of a business, within the relevant period or scale of production.

   a. Cost allocation
   b. Transaction cost
   c. Cost of quality
   d. Fixed costs

17. A _____ is a set of companies with interlocking business relationships and shareholdings. It is a type of business group.

The prototypical _____ are those which appeared in Japan during the 'economic miracle' following World War II.

   a. 1990 Clean Air Act
   b. 33 Strategies of War
   c. Keiretsu
   d. 28-hour day

18. _____ is a recursive process where two or more people or organizations work together in an intersection of common goals -- for example, an intellectual endeavor that is creative in nature--by sharing knowledge, learning and building consensus. _____ does not require leadership and can sometimes bring better results through decentralization and egalitarianism. In particular, teams that work collaboratively can obtain greater resources, recognition and reward when facing competition for finite resources._____ is also present in opposing goals exhibiting the notion of adversarial _____, though this is not a common case for using the term.

   a. Collectivism
   b. 28-hour day
   c. Collaboration
   d. 1990 Clean Air Act

19. _____ (NYSE: DE) is an American corporation based in Moline, Illinois, and the leading manufacturer of agricultural machinery in the world. In 2008, it was listed as 102nd in the Fortune 500 ranking. Deere and Company agricultural products, usually sold under the John Deere name, include tractors, combine harvesters, balers, planters/seeders, ATVs and forestry equipment.

a. 28-hour day
b. Deere ' Company
c. 1990 Clean Air Act
d. 33 Strategies of War

Chapter 7. Building Multidimensional Capabilities: The Management Challenge

1. _____ denotes the location where most, if not all, of the important functions of an organization are coordinated. The corporate _____ is the entity at the top of a corporation taking full responsibility managing all business activities. In the UK, the term 'head office' is most commonly used for the HQs of large corporations.
   a. Command center
   b. Headquarters
   c. Wells Fargo ' Co.
   d. National Center for Trauma-Informed Care

2. _____ is subcontracting a process, such as product design or manufacturing, to a third-party company. The decision to outsource is often made in the interest of lowering cost or making better use of time and energy costs, redirecting or conserving energy directed at the competencies of a particular business, or to make more efficient use of land, labor, capital, (information) technology and resources. _____ became part of the business lexicon during the 1980s.
   a. Opinion leadership
   b. Unemployment insurance
   c. Operant conditioning
   d. Outsourcing

3. An _____ is a person who has possession of an enterprise and assumes significant accountability for the inherent risks and the outcome. It is an ambitious leader who combines land, labor, and capital to create and market new goods or services. The term is a loanword from French and was first defined by the Irish economist Richard Cantillon.
   a. A4e
   b. A Stake in the Outcome
   c. AAAI
   d. Entrepreneur

4. _____ refers to the movement of cash into or out of a business or financial product. It is usually measured during a specified, finite period of time. Measurement of _____ can be used

   - to determine a project's rate of return or value. The time of _____s into and out of projects are used as inputs in financial models such as internal rate of return, and net present value.
   - to determine problems with a business's liquidity. Being profitable does not necessarily mean being liquid. A company can fail because of a shortage of cash, even while profitable.
   - as an alternate measure of a business's profits when it is believed that accrual accounting concepts do not represent economic realities. For example, a company may be notionally profitable but generating little operational cash (as may be the case for a company that barters its products rather than selling for cash.) In such a case, the company may be deriving additional operating cash by issuing shares evaluating default risk, re-investment requirements, etc.

   _____ is a generic term used differently depending on the context. It may be defined by users for their own purposes.

Chapter 7. Building Multidimensional Capabilities: The Management Challenge   49

a. Cash flow
b. Gross profit
c. Sweat equity
d. Gross profit margin

5. A _____ is a formal statement of a set of business goals, the reasons why they are believed attainable, and the plan for reaching those goals. It may also contain background information about the organization or team attempting to reach those goals.

The business goals may be defined for for-profit or for non-profit organizations.

a. Distributed management
b. Business plan
c. Time management
d. Crisis management

6. A _____, in business matters, is an entity that is controlled by a bigger and more powerful entity. The controlled entity is called a company, corporation, or limited liability company and in some cases can be a government or state-owned enterprise, and the controlling entity is called its parent (or the parent company.) The reason for this distinction is that a lone company cannot be a _____ of any organization; only an entity representing a legal fiction as a separate entity can be a _____.

a. 1990 Clean Air Act
b. 33 Strategies of War
c. Subsidiary
d. 28-hour day

7. In economics, business, retail, and accounting, a _____ is the value of money that has been used up to produce something, and hence is not available for use anymore. In economics, a _____ is an alternative that is given up as a result of a decision. In business, the _____ may be one of acquisition, in which case the amount of money expended to acquire it is counted as _____.

a. Cost allocation
b. Fixed costs
c. Cost overrun
d. Cost

50 *Chapter 7. Building Multidimensional Capabilities: The Management Challenge*

8. Procter is a surname, and may also refer to:

   - Bryan Waller Procter (pseud. Barry Cornwall), English poet
   - Goodwin Procter, American law firm
   - _____, consumer products multinational

   a. Strict liability
   b. Master and Servant Acts
   c. Downstream
   d. Procter ' Gamble

9. A _____ strategy targets non-buying customers in currently targeted segments. It also targets new customers in new segments. (Winer)

   A marketing manager has to think about the following questions before implementing a _____ strategy: Is it profitable? Will it require the introduction of new or modified products? Is the customer and channel well enough researched and understood?

   The marketing manager uses these four groups to give more focus to the market segment decision: existing customers, competitor customers, non-buying in current segments, new segments.

   a. Product line
   b. Context analysis
   c. Customer relationship management
   d. Market development

10. _____ is, in very basic words, a position a firm occupies against its competitors.

   According to Michael Porter, the three methods for creating a sustainable _____ are through:

   1. Cost leadership

   2. Differentiation

   3. Focus (economics)

a. 28-hour day
b. 1990 Clean Air Act
c. Theory Z
d. Competitive advantage

11. Competitive advantage is, in very basic words, a position a firm occupies against its competitors.

According to Michael Porter, the three methods for creating a _____ are through:

1. Cost leadership - Cost advantage occurs when a firm delivers the same services as its competitors but at a lower cost;

2.

a. 1990 Clean Air Act
b. 28-hour day
c. Sustainable Competitive advantage
d. Theory Z

Chapter 8. Preparing for the Future: Evolution of the Transnational

1. A _____ or transnational corporation is a corporation or enterprise that manages production or delivers services in more than one country. It can also be referred to as an international corporation.

   The first modern _____ is generally thought to be the Dutch East India Company, established in 1602.

   a. Multinational corporation
   b. Financial Accounting Standards Board
   c. Command center
   d. Small and medium enterprises

2. _____ generally refers to a list of all planned expenses and revenues. It is a plan for saving and spending. A _____ is an important concept in microeconomics, which uses a _____ line to illustrate the trade-offs between two or more goods.
   a. 28-hour day
   b. 33 Strategies of War
   c. 1990 Clean Air Act
   d. Budget

3. A _____ is a brief written statement of the purpose of a company or organization. Ideally, a _____ guides the actions of the organization, spells out its overall goal, provides a sense of direction, and guides decision making for all levels of management.

   _____s often contain the following:

   - Purpose and aim of the organization
   - The organization's primary stakeholders: clients, stockholders, etc.
   - Responsibilities of the organization toward these stakeholders
   - Products and services offered

   In developing a _____:

   - Encourage as much input as feasible from employees, volunteers, and other stakeholders
   - Publicize it broadly

   The _____ can be used to resolve differences between business stakeholders. Stakeholders include: employees including managers and executives, stockholders, board of directors, customers, suppliers, distributors, creditors, governments (local, state, federal, etc.), unions, competitors, NGO's, and the general public.

Chapter 8. Preparing for the Future: Evolution of the Transnational

a. 1990 Clean Air Act
b. Mission statement
c. 33 Strategies of War
d. 28-hour day

4. _____ is understood as a business unit within the overall corporate identity which is distinguishable from other business because it serves a defined external market where management can conduct strategic planning in relation to products and markets. When companies become really large, they are best thought of as being composed of a number of businesses (or _____s.)

In the broader domain of strategic management, the phrase '_____' came into use in the 1960s, largely as a result of General Electric's many units.

a. Strategic group
b. Strategic drift
c. Switching cost
d. Strategic business unit

5. 'Speaking generally, properties are those physical quantities which directly describe the physical attributes of the system; _____s are those combinations of the properties which suffice to determine the response of the system. Properties can have all sorts of dimensions, depending upon the system being considered; _____s are dimensionless, or have the dimension of time or its reciprocal.'

The term can also be used in engineering contexts, however, as it is typically used in the physical sciences.

When the terms formal _____ and actual _____ are used, they generally correspond with the definitions used in computer science.

a. 28-hour day
b. 1990 Clean Air Act
c. 33 Strategies of War
d. Parameter

6. _____ is one of the managerial functions like planning, organizing, staffing and directing. It is an important function because it helps to check the errors and to take the corrective action so that deviation from standards are minimized and stated goals of the organization are achieved in desired manner. According to modern concepts, _____ is a foreseeing action whereas earlier concept of _____ was used only when errors were detected. _____ in management means setting standards, measuring actual performance and taking corrective action.

Chapter 8. Preparing for the Future: Evolution of the Transnational

   a. Control
   b. Decision tree pruning
   c. Schedule of reinforcement
   d. Turnover

7. _____ is used to assign the available resources in an economic way. It is part of resource management.

In strategic planning, is a plan for using available resources, for example human resources, especially in the near term, to achieve goals for the future.

   a. 1990 Clean Air Act
   b. Resource allocation
   c. 33 Strategies of War
   d. 28-hour day

8. A _____ is a generalization of the Poisson process. In essence, the Poisson process is a continuous-time Markov process on the positive integers (usually starting at zero) which has independent identically distributed holding times at each integer i (exponentially distributed) before advancing (with probability 1) to the next integer: i + 1. In the same informal spirit, we may define a _____ to be the same thing, except that the holding times take on a more general distribution.
   a. Hausdorff moment problem
   b. SIPTA
   c. Markov chain
   d. Renewal process

9. _____ refers to the stock of skills and knowledge embodied in the ability to perform labor so as to produce economic value. It is the skills and knowledge gained by a worker through education and experience. Many early economic theories refer to it simply as labor, one of three factors of production, and consider it to be a fungible resource -- homogeneous and easily interchangeable.
   a. Market structure
   b. Deflation
   c. Productivity management
   d. Human capital

10. A _____ is the belief that there is a technique, method, process, activity, incentive or reward that is more effective at delivering a particular outcome than any other technique, method, process, etc. The idea is that with proper processes, checks, and testing, a desired outcome can be delivered with fewer problems and unforeseen complications. _____s can also be defined as the most efficient (least amount of effort) and effective (best results) way of accomplishing a task, based on repeatable procedures that have proven themselves over time for large numbers of people.

Chapter 8. Preparing for the Future: Evolution of the Transnational

a. Fix it twice
b. Best Practice
c. Hierarchical organization
d. Design management

11. _____ is the corporate management term for the act of reorganizing the legal, ownership, operational, or other structures of a company for the purpose of making it more profitable, or better organized for its present needs. Alternate reasons for _____ include a change of ownership or ownership structure, demerger repositioning debt _____ and financial _____.
  a. Restructuring
  b. Net worth
  c. Market value added
  d. Market value

12. _____ is an advertisement in which a particular product specifically mentions a competitor by name for the express purpose of showing why the competitor is inferior to the product naming it.

This should not be confused with parody advertisements, where a fictional product is being advertised for the purpose of poking fun at the particular advertisement, nor should it be confused with the use of a coined brand name for the purpose of comparing the product without actually naming an actual competitor. ('Wikipedia tastes better and is less filling than the Encyclopedia Galactica.')

In the 1980s, during what has been referred to as the cola wars, soft-drink manufacturer Pepsi ran a series of advertisements where people, caught on hidden camera, in a blind taste test, chose Pepsi over rival Coca-Cola.

  a. Comparative advertising
  b. 33 Strategies of War
  c. 1990 Clean Air Act
  d. 28-hour day

13. _____ is a business management strategy, initially implemented by Motorola, that today enjoys widespread application in many sectors of industry.

_____ seeks to improve the quality of process outputs by identifying and removing the causes of defects (errors) and variation in manufacturing and business processes. It uses a set of quality management methods, including statistical methods, and creates a special infrastructure of people within the organization ('Black Belts' etc.)

a. Theory of constraints
b. Takt time
c. Production line
d. Six sigma

14. _____ has been described as the 'process of social influence in which one person can enlist the aid and support of others in the accomplishment of a common task'. A definition more inclusive of followers comes from Alan Keith of Genentech who said '_____ is ultimately about creating a way for people to contribute to making something extraordinary happen.'

_____ is one of the most salient aspects of the organizational context. However, defining _____ has been challenging.

a. Situational leadership
b. Leadership
c. 28-hour day
d. 1990 Clean Air Act

15. The phrase mergers and _____s refers to the aspect of corporate strategy, corporate finance and management dealing with the buying, selling and combining of different companies that can aid, finance, or help a growing company in a given industry grow rapidly without having to create another business entity.

An _____, also known as a takeover or a buyout, is the buying of one company (the 'target') by another. An _____ may be friendly or hostile.

a. A4e
b. AAAI
c. A Stake in the Outcome
d. Acquisition

16. In economics and game theory, _____ are games of incomplete information where players receive possibly-correlated signals of the underlying state of the world. _____ were originally defined by Carlsson and van Damme (1993.) The most important practical application of _____ has been the study of crises in financial markets such as bank runs, currency crises, and bubbles.

a. Global games
b. Transferable utility
c. Perfect information
d. Mixed strategy

Chapter 8. Preparing for the Future: Evolution of the Transnational

17. _____ is the process of sharing of skills, knowledge, technologies, methods of manufacturing, samples of manufacturing and facilities among governments and other institutions to ensure that scientific and technological developments are accessible to a wider range of users who can then further develop and exploit the technology into new products, processes, applications, materials or services. It is closely related to (and may arguably be considered a subset of) Knowledge transfer. Related terms, used almost synonymously, include 'technology valorisation' and 'technology commercialisation'.
    a. Munn v. Illinois
    b. Competition law
    c. Mediation
    d. Technology transfer

18. In business, the term word _____ refers to a number of procurement practices, aimed at finding, evaluating and engaging suppliers of goods and services:

    - Global _____, a procurement strategy aimed at exploiting global efficiencies in production
    - Strategic _____, a component of supply chain management, for improving and re-evaluating purchasing activities
    - _____, the identification of job candidates through proactive recruiting technique
    - Co-_____, a type of auditing service
    - Low-cost country _____, a procurement strategy for acquiring materials from countries with lower labour and production costs in order to cut operating expenses
    - Corporate _____, a supply chain, purchasing/procurement, and inventory function
    - Second-tier _____, a practice of rewarding suppliers for attempting to achieve minority-owned business spending goals of their customer
    - Netsourcing, a practice of utilizing an established group of businesses, individuals, or hardware ' software applications to streamline or initiate procurement practices by tapping in to and working through a third party provider
    - Inverted _____, a price volatility reduction strategy usually conducted by procurement or supply-chain person by which the value of an organization's waste-stream is maximized by actively seeking out the highest price possible from a range of potential buyers exploiting price trends and other market factors
    - Multisourcing, a strategy that treats a given function, such as IT, as a portfolio of activities, some of which should be outsourced and others of which should be performed by internal staff.
    - Crowdsourcing, using an undefined, generally large group of people or community in the form of an open call to perform a task

In journalism, it can also refer to:

    - Journalism _____, the practice of identifying a person or publication that gives information
    - Single _____, the reuse of content in publishing

In computing, it can refer to:

- Open-_____, the act of releasing previously proprietary software under an open source/free software license
- Power _____ equipment, network devices that will provide power in a Power over Ethernet (PoE) setup

a. Cost Management
b. Reinforcement
c. Continuous
d. Sourcing

ANSWER KEY

Chapter 1
1. d   2. d   3. d   4. c   5. d   6. b   7. a   8. d   9. d   10. d
11. d   12. d

Chapter 2
1. b   2. b   3. c   4. a   5. d   6. b   7. a   8. d   9. c   10. d
11. d   12. d   13. d   14. d   15. b   16. d   17. d   18. a   19. d   20. d
21. a   22. d   23. b   24. c   25. d   26. d   27. d   28. b   29. a   30. b
31. a   32. b   33. c   34. d   35. d   36. d

Chapter 3
1. a   2. d   3. d   4. d   5. d   6. d   7. a   8. c   9. d   10. a
11. d   12. d   13. b   14. d   15. b   16. d   17. d   18. b   19. d   20. d
21. d   22. d   23. d   24. a   25. b   26. d   27. c   28. d   29. a   30. d
31. c   32. d   33. a   34. d

Chapter 4
1. b   2. d   3. a   4. d   5. c   6. c   7. b   8. d   9. d   10. d
11. d   12. d   13. c   14. d   15. d   16. d   17. d   18. a

Chapter 5
1. c   2. d   3. d   4. d   5. a   6. d   7. d   8. d   9. a   10. d
11. d   12. d   13. a   14. d   15. d   16. c   17. b   18. c   19. b   20. d
21. a   22. a   23. c

Chapter 6
1. b   2. d   3. c   4. d   5. d   6. d   7. d   8. a   9. d   10. d
11. d   12. c   13. b   14. a   15. d   16. d   17. c   18. c   19. b

Chapter 7
1. b   2. d   3. d   4. a   5. b   6. c   7. d   8. d   9. d   10. d
11. c

Chapter 8
1. a   2. d   3. b   4. d   5. d   6. a   7. b   8. d   9. d   10. b
11. a   12. a   13. d   14. b   15. d   16. a   17. d   18. d

www.ingramcontent.com/pod-product-compliance
Lightning Source LLC
Chambersburg PA
CBHW081219230426
43666CB00015B/2806